I Can Multiply, It's Not a Lie!

Tracy Kompelien

Consulting Editors, Diane Craig, M.A./Reading Specialist
and Susan Kosel, M.A. Education

Published by ABDO Publishing Company, 4940 Viking Drive, Edina, Minnesota 55435.

Printed in the United States.

Credits
Edited by: Pam Price
Curriculum Coordinator: Nancy Tuminelly
Cover and Interior Design and Production: Mighty Media
Photo Credits: ShutterStock, Wewerka Photography

Library of Congress Cataloging-in-Publication Data

Kompelien, Tracy, 1975-
  I can multiply, it's not a lie! / Tracy Kompelien.
   p. cm. -- (Math made fun)
  ISBN 10 1-59928-521-5 (hardcover)
  ISBN 10 1-59928-522-3 (paperback)

  ISBN 13 978-1-59928-521-4 (hardcover)
  ISBN 13 978-1-59928-522-1 (paperback)
  1. Multiplication--Juvenile literature. I. Title. II. Series.

QA115.K6635 2006
513.2'13--dc22

                                                                2006017375

SandCastle Level: Transitional

SandCastle™ books are created by a professional team of educators, reading specialists, and content developers around five essential components—phonemic awareness, phonics, vocabulary, text comprehension, and fluency—to assist young readers as they develop reading skills and strategies and increase their general knowledge. All books are written, reviewed, and leveled for guided reading, early reading intervention, and Accelerated Reader® programs for use in shared, guided, and independent reading and writing activities to support a balanced approach to literacy instruction. The SandCastle™ series has four levels that correspond to early literacy development. The levels help teachers and parents select appropriate books for young readers.

Emerging Readers
(no flags)

Beginning Readers
(1 flag)

Transitional Readers
(2 flags)

Fluent Readers
(3 flags)

These levels are meant only as a guide. All levels are subject to change.

To multiply is

to add a number to itself several times to find a total number. You can think of multiplication as repeated addition.

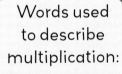

Words used to describe multiplication:

equal   product
factor   set
group   times

Here is a group of .

These  are a group of 3.

These are a set of 2.

These 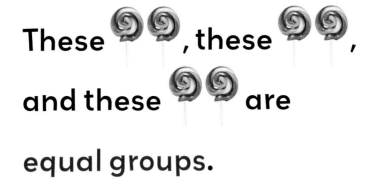, these , and these are

equal groups.

Multiplying is like adding a number to itself a certain number of times.
For example,
$2 + 2 + 2 = 6$
and $3 \times 2 = 6$

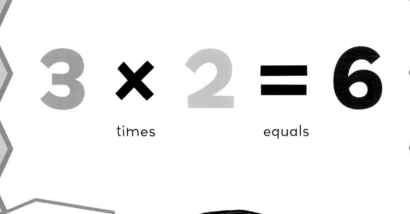

$$3 \times 2 = 6$$

times   equals

There are two ways to write the number sentence for 3 times 2 equals 6.

$$3 \quad \text{factor}$$

$$\times 2 \quad \text{factor}$$

$$6 \quad \text{product}$$

I Can Multiply, It's Not a Lie!

Sly is a hungry guy.
A carton of eggs
catches his eye.

How many eggs
are there to fix?
There are 2 rows of 6.
Sly can multiply!
He comes up with 12
and says, "Oh my!"

fourteen
14

Sly gives 2 of
the eggs a fry.
He can multiply,
and that is no lie!

Multiplying Every Day!

I will bake some muffins. My muffin tray has 3 rows of 4. I know that 3 times 4 equals 12.

3 × 4 = 12
muffins

eighteen
18

I have 3 groups of tomatoes. There are 5 tomatoes in each group. When I multiply 3 times 5, I find that I have 15 tomatoes.

3 x 5 = 15 tomatoes

There are 7 flowers in each bunch. I have 2 bunches, so that means I have 14 flowers!

I know that I have 2 groups of 7 each, which equals 14.
$2 \times 7 = 14$ flowers

I have 2 jars with 3 butterflies in each. Can you tell how many butterflies I have?

Glossary

equal – having exactly the same size or amount.

factor – one of the numbers that is multiplied to find the answer to a multiplication problem.

group – a collection of things put together in one unit, especially things that have something in common.

product – the answer to a multiplication problem.

set – two or more things that belong together or are used together.